Homosexuality: The Body or the Mind?

Homosexuality:
The Body or the Mind?

The Somatopsychology of Homosexuality

Mayetta L. Ford

VANTAGE PRESS
New York

The views expressed by the author are not necessarily those of the publisher. The publisher may not be held responsible for the opinions related in this work.

The author wishes to acknowledge permission to use the following:
Excerpts from *Modern Medical Guide* by Dr. Shyrock, copyright © 1979 by Pacific Press Publishing Association. Reprinted by permission.
Excerpts from *Human Genetics* by Norman V. Rothwell, copyright © 1977 by Prentice-Hall, Inc. Reprinted by permission.
Excerpts from *Psychology and Life* by Floyd L. Ruch, copyright © by Scott, Foresman, & Co. Reprinted by permission.
Excerpts from *Sex Hormones: Why Males and Females Are Different* by Caroline Arnold, copyright © 1981 by William Morrow & Company. Reprinted by permission.

Published by Vantage Press, Inc.
516 West 34th Street, New York, New York 10001

Manufactured in the United States of America
ISBN: 0-533-09352-X

Library of Congress Catalog Card No.: 90-91376

0 9 8 7 6 5 4 3 2 1

Dedicated to all persons (present and past) who have suffered because of the lack of knowledge and human understanding concerning one's fellowman.

Contents

Preface

It was twenty-seven years ago when, in conference with her "minor" professor, the author was informed that the time had come for her to select a topic for her thesis. Knowing that a thesis had to be presented to the faculty of graduate school as a partial fulfillment for the Master of Science degree in the field of psychology, she had already chosen her subject—homosexuality. However, the professor did not accept it, saying that the research would take too long. He advised her to begin research on homosexuality and later write the book.

The professor was right. During that time the gay world was a closed world. No person would dare admit this sexual orientation because of the stigma that society placed upon it and the problems it would engender for the individual.

The author turned to literature, but each book found was written by psychiatrists, doctors, psychologists, et cetera. These books told of "cases" they once had, and they treated the subject as an illness. They told of cases they had "cured," including what caused the individual to be homosexual. She could not be comfortable with what she read because it did not agree with what she had studied in the fields of human biology and genetics.

What disturbed this author most was the idea that sexuality could be chosen. Her reasoning could not come to grips with the idea that if an individual would (if such a thing were possible) choose a life that would make him/her suffer the "slings and arrows" of society and one's own family; a life that prohibited marriage to the object of one's love, and the impossibility of ever having a family and children with that love.

It was during the 60s and 70s when younger people who were not inhibited and "brainwashed" into following tradition began to "come out of the closet." It was too late for the older ones, many of whom were settled and pillars in their communities and churches. It was then when friends could be made and the topic could be discussed in an open, friendly, understanding way.

To those younger people this author owes a debt of gratitude for their help in making the writing of this treatise possible. Twenty-seven years after this author's discussion with her minor professor (using the null hypothesis as her guide in research), here is the book.

Homosexuality:
The Body or the Mind?

Introduction

The writing of this book is an attempt to shed some light on what can be called the most misunderstood, maligned, and mistakenly blamed condition of mankind—homosexuality. It is written in an effort to bring to the average person, especially those who have not had the privilege of study in the fields of genetics, psychology, endocrinology, and biological science and have the belief that an individual chooses his sexuality.

This belief is widespread to the extent that theologians and believers condemn to hell those who accept this sexual orientation. The justice system jails them; laws are written against them; jobs are withheld from them; many people fear them; families sometimes shun them; and many are harmed or even murdered because of it.

This writer hopes to present facts on this enigma and bring into focus the asininity of the beliefs and causes to which society adheres. She seeks to do this by bringing to the people information from the above-named fields of study with quotes from books written by authorities in their specific fields—people who have studied, researched, and carried out experiments; doctors who know the human body; psychologists who have made case studies, et cetera, and others who do not have to guess but *know* of what they speak.

The writer is greatly appreciative of the persons who gave her the permission to use their material as she tries to bring together between the covers of one book the information that is found in many books.

1

The reader will find that this book is written a bit differently from what is considered the formal way (i.e., with no footnotes). However, credit is given to those whose works are used.

It is hoped that when people have read this book, those who believe in "the choosing of sex" theory will

1. become enlightened and realize that persons of this segment of the world's population became what they are sexually just as every heterosexual did;

2. no longer blame their fellowmen but feel compassion;

3. (to somewhat paraphrase Martin Luther King, Jr.) judge them not for their sexuality but for the content of their character and their contribution to the culture;

4. have better attitudes toward humanity everywhere.

If this writer accomplishes the above and leads society to understand and change its attitude, the twenty-seven years of intermittent work will not have been in vain.

Chapter I
Society's Perceptions

When one listens to TV programs, such as "Donahue," "Sally Jessie Raphael," and "The Oprah Winfrey Show," concerning homosexuality; when one listens to ministers, et al., preach on the "sin" of homosexuality and damn those who "commit" it into hell; when one hears people in the audience scream at homosexual panels and refer to them as people who "chose" their sexual life; when persons, psychiatrists especially, speak of curing homosexuality; when people, such as those in Durham, North Carolina, collect thousands of signatures on a petition to oust the mayor because he dared to say that homosexuals have rights; when parents refuse to let their children be taught by a homosexual because they are afraid their children will be "turned into one"; when police go into a private bedroom (in a country that emphasizes human rights and is definitely against invasion of privacy) and arrest two consenting adults because they were engaging in an uncondoned kind of sex; when the homosexual sex act is referred to as a "crime against nature"; when people are sentenced to jail for it while many murderers and rapists go free; et cetera, et cetera, et cetera; one's mind goes back in history when, because of ignorance, mentally ill persons were cast into dungeons and bound in chains because they were "possessed of demons" and people in this country were killed because "they were witches" (during the Salem Madness of 1692, forty persons in Salem, Massachusetts, were put to death). One might

remember Joan of Arc, who declared that she heard heavenly voices commanding her to liberate her country, France, from foreign invaders. She was thought to be insane, but after a time was entrusted with the leadership and was successful; however she was later burned at the stake as a witch. This type of action was taken by people who thought they were doing right—people who knew no better.

In those days science had not advanced to half of what it is today, and much was not generally known (at least history doesn't record) such as the general nature of human growth and development, the dynamics of human behavior, or how the pattern of the individual person differentiates itself from others. It is possible that they were unaware of the composition of the human body beyond blood, flesh, and bones. Cells, hormones, genes, the organ systems of the body, and the interactions of these systems, were, no doubt, unknown to them (but they did speak of "humors" and their effects on personality). How one embryo developed into a male and another into a female was beyond their comprehension; hence, to a degree, their behavior can be understood because they knew no better. But today we live in a space age, and scientific knowledge has developed to a level never dreamed of by many. It is manifested in every aspect of our living and in our exploration of space to the degree that we have been successful in having a man walk on the moon. Gone are the days of the dungeons, chains, the burning at the stake, et cetera, but one thing that remains from those bygone days of centuries ago is man's inhumanity to man.

Today, science has revealed to man things that put in focus how wrong those people were. Yet, in spite of the knowledge of the science that we have today and our dedication to human rights, there is a a segment of the population that is persecuted, prosecuted, denied human rights and jobs, scorned and, in

many instances, hurt or killed because their sexual orientation is different from what society considers normal.

It is now known how an individual comes into being to the extent that we have been able to produce test-tube babies. It is known what makes us "tick," what body chemistry is, how it works—but not why. One has no control over body chemistry, for it has a "mind" of its own, so to speak. One does not love a certain individual simply because one wants to; one loves because one cannot control it. Body chemistry dictates that. Neither can one make himself love an individual because the individual loves him regardless of what he does for him. Body chemistry dictates that. Yet, those whose body chemistries respond to other people than their opposite sex are targets for discrimination. Because of society's beliefs, they are considered by some as immoral sinners on the way to hell. Some of them even bear the scorn of their own families.

In the heterosexual, body chemistry reacts to the opposite sex, and physically one's own sex is sexually repulsive to him or her. Thus, the thought of a person "allowing" or "choosing" this to happen arouses the same feeling in them. This idea is pervasive and is used as the main factor for the negativity of the nongay society. People are aware that when one (gay or nongay) reaches a certain age, one goes into puberty. The pituitary gland releases a hormone (or hormones) that awaken the internal sex glands which have lain dormant heretofore. The body begins to take on a more grown-up look. This is when the body chemistry reacts or does not react to the opposite sex, and this is beyond the person's control. There is only one difference between the heterosexual and the homosexual, and that is the object (meaning, person) that arouses the reaction. Arousal comes to both alike, and it feels alike even to people of differing orientation.

It is difficult for the general public to understand that what it feels and thinks it knows about homosexuals and

homosexuality is false "information" received from others who received *their* information from others. In practically all cases, none of those passing it on to others are certain that it is true. If called upon, they could not support their statements.

It is hard to believe that doctors do not know that to some extent the homosexual body composition is a bit different from the heterosexual's, yet they do not make it known to courts and those who are responsible for insuring individual human rights.

Below is an article that appeared in *Medical Abstracts Newsletter* for November 1986 (volume 6, number 12). The appearance of this article in *Medical Abstracts Newsletter* gives truth to the fact that it is known by many that chromatin of the opposite sex can be found in some individuals and that its existence can cause a degree of masculization in females and, conversely so, feminization in males. However, it seems that many do not link this to sexual orientation.

GENDER TESTS FOR WOMEN ATHLETES: NEW CRITICISM

The International Olympics Committee requires female participants to undergo a gender verification test to determine if they have Y (male) chromatin in their genetic makeup, which could produce male body structure and added muscle. According to this report, however, some women who show only X (female) chromatin may have other genetic abnormalities that cause masculinization. Conversely, some women found to have Y chromatin don't have any signs of masculinization. Therefore, the author concludes that currently used screening tests are inaccurate and discriminatory. (A. de la Chapelle in *Journal of American Medical Assn.* 256: 1920, Oct. 1986.)

The X and Y chromosomes will be dealt with in detail later when how sex is determined is discussed.

Because those who know remain silent to a great degree about the truth, they allow society (in which the negativity is existent) to go on believing false explanations as to the possible etiology of homosexuality. Below are some of the views expressed and believed by a vast majority of society (as strange as they may seem).

1. When parents allow a child to play with toys identified with the opposite sex, such as a boy playing with dolls, he becomes gay.
2. When parents have a child opposite to the sex they wanted and raise him/her as the sex they wanted, he/she becomes gay.
3. If a homosexual teaches one's child, the child will be "turned into a homosexual."
4. All homosexuals molest children.
5. It's all in the mind and can be cured.
6. A homosexual can be compelled to not be "that way."
7. Homosexuals are men and women who have low morals and will attack heterosexuals if given a chance.
   And the list goes on . . .

In her book *Child Development* (p. 38), Elizabeth Hurlock, Ph.D., associate in psychology at the graduate school of the University of Pennsylvania, tells us that there is no known way of changing the hereditary endowment of an individual after the moment of conception. If that be true (and it is an accepted fact by science), then it goes without saying that a homosexual cannot be changed to a heterosexual any more than heterosexual can be changed to a homosexual. She verifies that many children show these characteristics long before they know anything about sex or the existence of the sex act.

There are cases where a homosexual person has supposedly been "cured" and is now heterosexual, but what has happened here is that the individual was not a true homosexual, but was bisexual in the beginning and now he has been awakened to this. These are those who have gone to psychiatrists because society has led them to believe that it's in the mind. Yes, he may now have sexual feelings for the opposite sex awakened, but that same drive that was there first remains and will still surface. He may say he is cured, but this is done to get the psychiatrist and society "off his back," and he can now escape the scorn and harassment of society. He can now have a family and live an accepted life on the surface.

Below is an article from page 23 of the January 27, 1987, issue of *Weekly World News*. The entire article is presented (reprinted by permission).

ONCE A SISSY—ALWAYS A SISSY, SAYS TOP SHRINK

At last research has confirmed what everyone knew all along—little "sissy" boys grow up to be homosexuals.

According to a study by UCLA's Dr. Richard Green, most boys who show effeminate behavior early on will wind up loving men instead of women, no matter what kind of therapy or child-rearing practices they are exposed to in childhood.

Dr. Green, a noted psychiatrist and sex researcher, studied 44 extremely feminine boys from the time they were little children until they became adult men. In the 15 years his study lasted, he found that three-quarters of his subjects matured as homosexuals or bisexuals.

Green concluded that some youngsters have an inborn "receptivity" to influence in their environment that can encourage a homosexual orientation.

Exhibited in this article is a fact that seems to prevail in the thinking of many. Notice that in the last paragraph, although the preceding paragraphs confirm the title of the article and the fact that the characteristics are inborn, Dr. Green continues to blame the environment "that can encourage a homosexual orientation." He somewhat disputes himself in the second paragraph concerning the use of therapy and environmental influences.

It is an accepted fact that an individual is a product of his/her inheritance and his/her environment. A simple explanation of this is that one's heredity determines to what heights one can go (i.e., potential) and the environment determines to what degree that potential comes to a realization.

Often the argument here is that there are people from poor environments who sometimes rise to unexpected heights and, conversely so, those from good environments who do just the opposite. In these cases, inheritance superseded environment in its effect; however, which exerts more influence remains a moot question.

Psychology tells us that behavior of every kind is an overt manifestation of an inward feeling (i.e., drive). Behavior can be defined as an overt manifestation resulting from the interaction of the psychophysical systems within the body as they, in turn, interact with the environment. In other words, whatever behavior one exhibits (if not forced) is precipitated by an inward feeling (i.e., urge) that is alleviated or satisfied by that behavior. Dr. Floyd L. Ruch, professor of psychology at the University of Southern California, corroborates this in his book *Psychology and Life* (page 17) thusly:

All psychological activity—human thinking, feeling, and doing—depends upon the biological functioning of the organism (body). Modern psychologists, in contrast to the early European philosophers, have come to look upon the mind and body as inseparable aspects of the total reacting organism.

9

Here Ruch puts forth the foundation upon which the definition of behavior stands, and one should realize that overt behavior is simply the action from a covert feeling. Where there is no feeling, there is no action (i.e., behavior). It begins within the body.

Chapter II
The Human Body

In the foreword of the book *Human Personality and Its Survival of Bodily Death,* by F. W. H. Myers, Aldous Huxley refers to the body as the house of the soul. However, this writer prefers to call it the machine in which we live, because the body is a most complex, finely tuned machine. It is a machine created by God and (shall we say) programmed by God with even the most minute function of its automatic systems timed to perfection. It stands to reason that since all psychological activity depends upon the functioning of the human body, if one is to understand behavior *per se* and patterns of behavior, one must know something of the body, how it functions and in what way behavior is influenced by its functions.

The quote below by Clarence G. Young, G. Ladyard Stebbins, and John Hylander in their book *The Human Organism and the World of Life: A Survey in Biological Science* (page 241) gives a good start to learning this and starts with the response system.

In human beings there is a highly developed response system composed of three parts.

1. The receptors, or sense organs, which specialize in sensitivity to stimulation;
2. The conductors, or nerves, which specialize in conducting stimulation from the sense organs to the effectors;

3. The effectors, or muscles and glands, which carry out the responses of the organism.

This book defines the glands as modified epithelial tissue. It is these glands that determine how the body "works" and much of its behavior after being programmed at the time of conception, especially the glands of the endocrine system. This is a system of glands called ductless glands because they pour their hormones directly into the blood system and not through special tubes. (The word hormone comes from the Greek word meaning "I excite.") Since the writer is not an authority on the human body, this chapter will contain much material from books by persons who are authorities in their respective fields.

In his book *Psychology and Life*, Floyd L. Ruch tell us that

> man is a product of his nature and his nurture—all that he is or ever will become is determined by his inheritance and his environment.—An individual's heredity endowment determined at the time of his conception has a great influence on biological and psychological characteristics as they later develop.—The process from a single one-celled organism into an adult being, with his many billions of cells and his remarkable physical and mental capacities, is wonderfully complex.

Although not "spelled out" specifically, here he alludes to something that often is not taken into consideration—the fact that there is more to humanity than a body. It was Richard Simmons, the exercise guru, who said, "God made people in all shapes, sizes, and packages. That's all the body is—packaging." Simply put, the person is in that packaging. To live in a tangible world, one must have a tangible body to exist in that world. The Christian religion teaches that at death, one leaves the body and enters another dimension. In other words, al-

12

though the body is dead, the individual (i.e., spirit) continues to live. There are millions who believe in reincarnation and believe that they have lived before. Thus, when one sees an individual, only the physical self is seen, but there also exists an emotional self, a spiritual self, a psychological self, et cetera, and so it follows that there is physical sex and psychological sex. In the homosexual, there appears to be a difference between the physical sex and the psychological sex. The body may be male, but the person may feel, think, and act female; to himself, he is female. This is often spoken of as a male in a female body or a female in a male body. Herein lies the mystery, the misunderstanding, the prejudice from which much of society's beliefs, fears, and reactions spring. In an attempt to unravel this, one must first know what happens at conception that determines physical sex. What causes one organism to develop male and another female? What programs the sperm and the egg to unite and produce either male or female?

Simply put, the female has an X chromosome and the male has an X and a Y chromosome. In the ejaculated sperm from the male, there are myriads of these minute X and Y tadpole-looking chromosomes that carry all the traits the child will inherit from the father. They swim toward the female egg, which carries only X chromosomes with the traits the child will inherit from the mother. If an X from the father penetrates the X egg, the resulting child will be a female. If a Y from the father penetrates the X egg, the child will be a male. At this point of conception, all one's hereditary endowment and traits (body structure, color of hair, eyes, sexuality, et cetera) are determined.

Mr. Ruch continues:

During conception, two living germ cells (the sperm from the

13

father and the egg, or ovum, from the mother) unite to produce an individual.

The male and the female germ cells, technically known as gametes, form a single cell called the zygote. Within both the sperm and the egg are reptile-like structures called chromosomes. The gametes are unique in that they contain only half the number of chromosomes found in other body cells. Thus, the zygote they form contains the normal number of chromosomes—half from the egg and half from the sperm.

Many lines of evidence from the field of Genetics leave little doubt that the determiners of a person's heredity characteristics are locked within the chromosomes. In each of them are ultramicroscopic areas called genes which are the real bearers of a person's heredity.

Please keep the chromosomes in mind, for therein may lie the answer to the question, "Are homosexuals born or are they made?" Does homosexuality have a physical (soma) or a mental (Psyche) etiology?

Mr. Ruch adds:

Since the fertilized egg receives exactly half of its chromosomes from the father and half from the mother, the child does not (despite popular belief) inherit more characteristics from the parent of *his own sex*. However, the characteristics of sex itself are determined by the *male gamete alone*. Whereas the sex-determining chromosomes of the female are all the same kind, called "X chromosomes," a *mature* male reproductive cell may contain either an X chromosome or a different kind called a "Y chromosome." *If a male sex cell containing an X chromosome fertilizes an ovum, the child will be a girl: if the male cell has a Y chromosome, the child will be a boy.*

(Think of Anne Boleyn who was beheaded by her spouse, King Henry VIII, because of her "inability" to give him a boy.)

One can not dispute the possibility of something going wrong here, and this gives rise to a few questions.

- Has anyone in the field of genetics given proven evidence that all X and all Y chromosomes of the male are absolute and perfect?
- Is it possible that an X from the male could have a bit of Y in it or a Y a bit of the X in it? If this should happen, would the resulting individual have a psychological sex different from the physical sex and thus a male have the body chemistry of a female and vice versa and thus be attracted to his/her "own sex"?

One's psychological sex is one's perceptions of one's self which results from the feelings, emotions, feminine or masculine characteristics which are natural to him/her. Although they may not be characteristic of the physical sex the individual feels that he is one of the opposite sex and his/her body chemistry reacts as that of the opposite sex (Floyd L. Ruch, *Psychology and Life*).

- Did the researchers, thinking that there were only two sexes, and having found the X and Y chromosomes, stop there? Is there a third chromosome not yet discovered?

These questions might seem asinine, but when one is searching for truth, every possibility should be explored. If these questions cannot be answered, another question rises: Should more research be done to find the answers?

Certain theologians and others might be quick to quote the scripture of Genesis, chapter I, verse 27 (the King James version), "So God created man in His own image, in the image of God created He him: male and *only* female created He them." It is true that He did, but the scripture does not say *only* male and *only* female created He them, or perfect male and female created He them.

Since the dawn of civilization (and perhaps before), almost all of humanity believed that the world was flat and that if one sailed to the edge, one could fall off. But in 1492, Columbus proved that premise wrong when he sailed from Europe in an attempt to reach the riches of the East by sailing west and found the new world. Likewise, man adhered to the geocentric theory expounded by Copernicus—that the Earth was the center of the universe, and the sun revolved around it. Even the Bible speaks of the day in the battle of Jericho when "the sun stood still," but, during the fifteenth century, there came an Italian scientist by the name of Galileo who proved that the sun is the center of the universe and the planets revolve around the sun. This caused the world to discard the geocentric theory and replace it with the heliocentric theory, which exists even today.

What does all of this have to do with sex? Simply this! Regardless of how prevalent a belief is, it can be wrong. It is time that the theory that there are only two sexes be discarded, when actually, there are six sexes—two dominant and four "in between" sexes.

1. male man   3. female man   5. bisexual man
2. female woman   4. male woman   6. bisexual woman

We all have seen men with feminine characteristics that are "opposite" their sex, such as the high pitched female voice (which comes from the size of vocal cords), the "fragile" emotions commonly associated with a female, the secondary characteristics of a woman, and often the facial features of a female—this, of course, in varying degrees. Did he "choose" this or is this a person who is psychologically female, but "born in the body of a male" (with some alterations)? Likewise we see the woman with masculine characteristics such as the wide shoulders of the male, the low male voice, androgynous facial features, and the secondary characteristics of a male. There are some females who must shave; some in whose family there is a male pattern baldness become bald; all of this is caused by hormones. If one were to go back into the childhoods of these individuals, there is a great possibility, in many cases, that as children these persons exhibited the characteristics of the "opposite" sex long before they knew that there was such a thing as sex.

One might think that those are the characteristics of all homosexuals. No, that is not what is being said here. This will be examined again later, and the emphasis will then be on the reason for these characteristics (the part that the hormones play). When one sees these characteristics, it is possible that the individual observed may be homosexual or heterosexual. Conversely, others without such characteristics may also be homosexual or heterosexual. This is brought to attention often so that one will be aware of this and should feel that there is some reason for it. The reader may reach his or her own conclusions.

On Sunday, July 1, 1985, there appeared in the Raleigh, North Carolina, *News and Observer* newspaper an article titled "True Physical Hermaphrodites Rare." It was written by Dr. June M. Reinesch, who cited the Kinsey Report as her authority. It appeared that Dr. Reinesch is also a columnist and was answering a letter that was written to her by a person who was concerned about a friend.

The person writing the letter told the doctor about a girl with whom she was sharing an apartment who referred to herself as an hermaphrodite. She showed her pubic area, and it did look as if there were small testicles in the vulva lips as well as a small penis. This, the roommate told the writer of the letter, caused her great embarrassment. The writer asked

Reinesch if her roommate was male or female; if she could become pregnant; how such a thing happened; and if the condition was hereditary.

Dr. Reinesch responded to the letter in the following way. She told the young woman that the idea that only two sexes exist is not true in the cases of many people. She spoke of the fact that only approximately two hundred cases had been verified in which a person had both male and female gonads (sex organs). In those cases, the person usually had a uterus and experienced breast development at the onset of puberty. Also, the menses appeared. However, because of the appearance of the genitalia (external sex organs) at birth that looked masculine, the child was thought to be male and was raised as a male.

So far, as true hermaphrodites are concerned, she continued, it is seldom that they produce sperm, although many have functioning ovaries that release eggs. In some cases there is a uterus and fallopian tubes, which suggests that pregnancy could be possible; however, there is only one documented case of a true hermaphrodite bearing a child.

Dr. Reinesch goes on to say that there are many types of "pseudo-hermaphrodites" or "intersex" people who have some of the characteristics of both sexes based on the evaluation of the reproductive organs, chromosomes, genitalia, and hormone levels, but that they have only one type of gonads (either ovaries or testicles), which matches their chromosomal sex, and also have genitalia that look like those of the opposite sex.

Then there is a type of "intersex" person who is androgen-insensitive. Here the individual has normal testicles, male chromosomes, and produces normal levels of testosterone, but the cells can't use the testosterone. (Androgen is a male hormone that can give rise to masculine characteristics.)

In these persons female genitalia are developed before

birth, and at puberty feminine development takes place. This is because their testicles also manufacture estrogen (a female hormone that stimulates the development of female characteristics), which is not counteracted by the effects of the testosterone, as would normally be done if the cells could use it. Only a few specific cases of this have been found, but it does not appear to "run in families"—not hereditary, she stated. There could be many more, but no statistics have been kept on this.

Continuing her response to the letter writer, Dr. Reinesch stated that although basically all humans start out the same (except for their chromosomes), the undifferentiated gonads develop according to the message they receive from the chromosomes. This means that whether the fetus develops male or female tissue depends upon the chromosomes.

Once the sex organs (gonads) become either male or female, both the internal reproductive organs and the external genitalia (organs) are controlled by many hormones of which testosterone is the most important. If it is present, male internal and external organs will devleop. If it is not present, female organs will develop. *This is a complicated process and can be disrupted at different stages of development resulting in individuals with all degrees of male and female characteristics, of reproductive organs, of external appearance, of hormone levels, and of sex chromosomes.*

Having thus spoken of different reasons that cause one's sex to be affected, the doctor gave advice on what the person so affected can do. Once her chromosomal sex has been established, her hormonal levels and the status of her internal organs also established, hormonal treatment can help her match her external appearance to her psychological sex. Also, plastic surgery can make her genitalia appear more female. Of course, the doctor was referring to the person about whom she was written.

19

Because of the relevancy of the information given in the article to the thesis of this manuscript, it is included; however, one should not misconstrue this and think that homosexuality means that the individual has such abnormalities. This information is *evidence that sex is not always clearly defined, not only psychological sex but physical sex also, and that physical sex does not always coincide with psychological sex. This was a case of a person with both physical sexes. In cases like this, deciding if a baby is a male or a female at birth often is a "game of chance."*

There is no "cut and dried" sexuality that fits all persons. With no evidence to refute Dr. Reinesch, one can conclude that if the classification of existing sexuality were to be depicted graphically, it would not lend itself to the dichotomous classification that society gives it, i.e., that one is either completely male or completely female. This being the case, then one can surmise that it is more of a continuum, with male at one pole and female at the other pole, and gradations by degree in between. Too, she brings forth the fact that there are instances when sex genitalia are not always completely male or completely female—or only male or only female.

However, her last two statements give rise to questions. There is doubt in this writer's mind that a true female or a true male can have his/her sex changed to the opposite by an operation, nor would he or she want this. Thus, there is no such thing as a "sex-change operation," the kind one often reads about in the newspaper. Without a doubt, the subject must have at least the rudiments of some abnormality with which the doctor can begin the change. In no true male or female, heterosexual or homosexual, are such abnormalities existent. There is a difference in homosexuality and the type of person described in the article. The doctor herself states (or implies) that there are more than two sexes. Degrees of certain sexuality seem to run the gamut of the continuum.

While doing research for this book, this writer tried very hard to get an interview with some surgeon to discuss sex-change operations, but was not successful. Those who were asked were reluctant to talk about it. The subject of erogenous zones will not be discussed here. Suffice it to say, there is a difference. Human beings are complex beings, and there are billions on earth with no two exactly the same in all aspects. Thus a specific pattern cannot be matched to a specific sexuality in most cases, although it can in some.

Chapter III
The Bible Comes In

"Opposites attract and likes repel." This is an adage that has stood the test of time and, like a law of nature, it will prevail. Perhaps this is why homosexuality is called "a crime against nature"; however, the same law applies there also—opposites attract, likes repel.

In the preceding chapter, it was stated that there are six sexes instead of only two as it has been heretofore believed. When such a categorization as this is made, one should be cognizant of the fact that there is a possibility that a variable is also operant—degrees. Nevertheless, if this is true here, it cannot be quantitatively determined and is therefore ignored. In order to avoid confusion, categories must be used.

The male and female sexes are the first two sexes. The bisexual male and bisexual female are the second two sexes, and the female male and the male female are the third two sexes.

First two sexes: The body chemistry of the male male and of the female female react to each other—opposites attracting.

Second two sexes: The body chemistry of the bisexual male reacts to femaleness whether it is in the female female or the female man, and the bisexual female's body chemistry reacts to maleness whether it is in the male or the male female (lesbian)—opposites attracting.

Third two sexes: The body chemistry of the male female reacts to femaleness whether it is in the bisexual female or the female female, and the body chemistry of the female male reacts to the maleness whether in the bisexual male or the male male—opposites attracting. There are never two female females; never two male males; never two female males, never two male females comprising a couple.

One wonders why a female male is sometimes killed or rebuffed in a saner manner when he makes sexual overtones to a male male. This is because the body chemistry of the male male causes him to feel repulsion. A female female experiences the same feeling as the male male when she is approached by a male female. She also feels repulsion. All of this is because the body chemistry repels; it is two magnets with the same polarity—like repelling like. Since body chemistry cannot be changed, then a homosexual cannot be changed into a heterosexual nor a heterosexual be changed into a homosexual.

No person (other than those involved in prostitution) voluntarily indulges in a sex act if his body chemistry does not react positively toward the other individual. There must be a drive (feeling, need) that the act can satisfy—a desire that comes from within the body; it is not "all in the head." One is born with it and one will die with it. This has been said before but needs to be repeated here.

If all that has been said is true, why were Sodom and Gomorrah destroyed because of homosexuality? The same question vexed this writer. In trying to find the answer, it was found that nowhere in the Bible does it say that the destruction was because of homosexuality, yet this "fact" is preached constantly by unlearned ministers and by some who have degrees in theology.

If one not accustomed to reading the Bible were to read it, one would find that many things preached are not true—simply because it is so often misinterpreted. So instead of just giving the book, the chapter, and the verses from which people cull the idea that Sodom and Gomorrah were destroyed because of homosexuality, the verses are printed here. This is for the convenience of the millions who do not read the Bible, including persons of religions that do not use the Bible; some have the Koran, and others have other holy books.

The following is taken from the King James Version of the Bible because it is the Bible that was translated directly from the Hebrew and Greek. It is the one to which references will be made throughout this study.

The evidence cited by theologians and all others who adhere to the theory that Sodom and Gomorrah were destroyed because of homosexuality records events that happened *after* God had promised to destroy the cities. It is found in Genesis, chapter 19, verses 4 and 5 that read thusly:

> But before they lay down, the men of the city, even the men of Sodom, compassed the house round, both old and young, all the people from every quarter:
> And they called unto Lot, and said unto him, Where are the men which came in to thee this night? bring them out unto us, that we may know them.

To get everything in the proper perspective, let us go back to chapter 18 of Genesis and read verses 20 through 33:

> And the Lord said, Because the cry of Sodom and Gomorrah is great, and because their sin is very grievous;
> I will go down now and see whether they have done altogether according to the cry of it, which is come unto me: and if not, I will know.
> And the men turned their faces from thence, and went

forward toward Sodom: but Abraham stood yet before the Lord.

And Abraham drew near and said, Wilt thou also destroy the righteous with the wicked?

Peradventure there be fifty righteous within the city: Wilt thou also destroy and not spare the fifty righteous that are therein?

That be far from thee to do after this manner; to slay the righteous with the wicked: and that the righteous should be as the wicked, that be far from thee: Shall the judge of all the earth do right?

And the Lord said, If I find in Sodom fifty righteous within the city, then I will spare all the place for their sakes.

And Abraham answered and said, Behold now, I have taken upon me to speak unto the Lord, which am but dust and ashes.

Peradventure there shall lack five of the fifty righteous; wilt thou destroy all the city for lack of five? And he said, If I find there forty and five, I will not destroy it.

And he spake unto him yet again, and said, Peradventure there shall be forty found there. And he said, I will not do it for forty's sake.

And he said unto him, Oh let not the Lord be angry, and I will speak: Peradventure there shall thirty be found there. And he said, I will not do it, if I find thirty there.

And he said, Behold now, I have taken upon me to speak unto the Lord: Peradventure there shall be twenty found there. And he said, I will not destroy it for twenty's sake.

And he said, Oh let not the Lord be angry, and I will speak yet but this once: Peradventure ten shall be found there. And he said, I will not destroy it for ten's sake.

And the Lord went his way, as soon as he had left communing with Abraham: and Abraham returned unto his place.

These verses document that it was after God had promised to destroy Sodom and Gomorrah if ten righteous couldn't be found, that the incident upon which people based their belief took place. The cities were already condemned and God had sent two angels, as indicated in Genesis, chapter 19, verses 1, 2, and 3:

And there came two angels to Sodom at even; and Lot sat in the gate of Sodom: And Lot seeing them rose up to meet them; and he bowed himself with this face toward the ground; And he said, Behold now, my lords, turn in, I pray you, into your servant's house, and tarry all night, and wash your feet, and ye shall rise up early, and go on your way. And they said, Nay, but we will abide in the street all night.

And he pressed upon them greatly; and they turned into his house, and he made them a feast, and did bake unleavened bread, and they did eat.

Here, it seems that the two angels whom God had sent to destroy Sodom were among the men that Lot was asked to send out to the callers. Nowhere in this chapter or any other does it say that the men were sent out or that the outside men ever reached them.

Look now at chapter 19 of Genesis, verses 9 through 13. Here Lot goes out to meet the men.

And they said, Stand Back. And they said again, This one fellow came in to sojourn, and he will needs be a judge: now will we deal worse with thee, than with them. And they pressed sore upon the man, even Lot, and came near to break the door.

But the men put forth their hand, and pulled Lot into the house to them, and shut the door.

And they smote the men that were at the door of the house with the blindness, both small and great; so that they wearied themselves to find the door.

And the men said unto Lot, Hast thou here any besides? son in law, and their sons, and their daughters, and whatsoever thou hast in the city, bring them out of this place:

For we will destroy this place, because the cry of them is waxen great before the face of the Lord and the Lord hath sent us to destroy it.

It was only after God promised to destroy Sodom and Gomorrah (in Genesis 18:20-33) that the incident in Genesis 19:4, 5 took place.

Now go to Ezekiel, chapter 16, and listen as God rebukes Israel for its wickedness and speaks of its many sins. In this chapter you will find God saying why he destroyed Sodom and Gomorrah.

V. 28 Thou hast played the whore also with the Assyrians, because thou wast unsatiable; yea, thou hast played the harlot with them, and yet couldest not be satisfied.

V. 48 As I live, saith the Lord God, Sodom thy sister hath not done, she nor her daughters, as thou hast done, thou and thy daughters.

V.49 Behold, this was the iniquity of thy sister Sodom, pride, fullness of bread, and abundance of idleness was in her and in her daughters, neither did she strengthen the hand of the poor and needy.

V. 50 And they were haughty, and committed abomination before me: therefore I took them away as I saw good.

V. 52 Thou also, which hast judged thy sisters, bear thine own shame for thy sins that thou hast committed more abominable than they: they are more righteous than thou: yea, be thou confounded also, and bear they shame, in that thou hast justified thy sisters.

V. 53 When I shall bring again their captivity, the captivity of

Sodom and her daughters, and the captivity of thy captives in the midst of them:

V. 55 When thy sisters, Sodom and her daughters, shall return to their former estate, and Samaria and her daughters shall return to their former estate, then thou and thy daughters shall return to your former estate.

Many Bibles have been printed since the King James Version, and much of the wording has changed, but the King James Version was the first translation. The second volume of the *New Standard Encyclopedia* from the Standard Education Society, Inc., of Chicago, Illinois, tells us the following:

Bible, the Scriptures, the Word is of Greek origin, signifying a book of books. Both meanings retained. ——In plural, the Bible is a library of the sacred literature of the Hebrews contained in sixty-six books. With the exception of a few chapters the thirty-nine books of the Old Testament were written originally in Hebrew. The twenty-seven books of the New Testament were written wholly in Greek.

To summarize this chapter:

1. Sodom and Gomorrah were not destroyed because of homosexuality;
2. Sodom and Gomorrah were destroyed because ten righteous people could not be found;
3. The incident that people use to prove that the cities were destroyed because of homosexuality is not followed by anything; nowhere in the Bible does it say that the act was carried out; rather—just the opposite—the men were blinded.

4. When God was speaking to the Israelites, he told them why the two cities were destroyed (Ezekiel 16:49, 50);
5. God told the Israelites that their sins were worse than the sins of Sodom and Gomorrah—that their sins were more *abominable*;
6. They would be treated the same as Sodom and Gomorrah when He brought their captivity.

Other questions that one might ask:

- Did the clergy who have preached the Sodom and Gomorrah destruction-for-homosexuality theory know all the while that they were preaching falsely?
- Did they do it because they wanted to say what people had said before them and knew it was what people wanted to hear and to which would respond favorably, or did they let their emotions take precedence over their intellect?

It is true that Sodom and Gomorrah were destroyed because of sin. It also seems to be true that homosexuality was going on there. However, it was not only in Sodom and Gomorrah. It has existed since time immemorial (perhaps before man came upon the Earth, because it exists in the animal world) and will continue to exist as long as life exists—that is, in the form of living fleshly organisms.

Chapter IV
The Endocrine System

Of the many systems of the body, the endocrine system is the most unique in that its internal secretions (i.e., hormones) are poured directly into the blood stream and reach the sight of their operation without ducts. It is known as the system with ductless glands and is often referred to as the computer programmed to run the machine that we call our bodies from before birth until death. However, all systems of the body must be integrated with each other in order that the body maintain homeostasis (balance). In order that this is maintained, each organ of the system must "know" the amount of hormones, the place of destination, and the time of release. When any of these conditions are not met, the normalcy of the body suffers and disorder occurs; thus (it has been found that) much overt behavior is determined by the functioning of this system. The internal sex glands belong to this system, and although this system and its workings are very complex, the quote below seems to sum up its importance and the power of the hormones that it secretes.

The book *Hormones, Sex, and Happiness*, written by Elizabeth B. Connell, M.D., Joseph E. Davis, M.D., Joseph Goldzielser, M.D., and Eleanor Z. Wallace, M.D., says this on the inside cover.

Medical science has long known human behavior is influenced by the ebb and flow of many tides, including the

30

hormonal tide. From birth to death, successive waves of hormones engulf us. When present in the right amounts, they nurture and sustain us. Out of control they drown us.

Most of the information concerning hormones has been learned by scientists in the last three decades. Endocrinology is practically a new branch of medical science.

Caroline Arnold, in her book *Sex Hormones—Why Males and Females Are Different*, has this to say on page 15:

> Hormones are found in all animals and even in some plants. Because the existence of hormones is so widespread, they probably appeared very early in the evolution of life. In the case of higher animals such as mammals and birds, they are produced by the endocrine glands.
>
> The endocrine glands that produce hormones involved in sex and reproduction are the pituitary, the adrenals, and the gonads (ovaries in the female, testes in the male).

The hormones of the pituitary (a very small gland at the base of the brain) act directly upon other endocrine glands and organs and stimulate them to produce other hormones. This causes changes in the production of sex hormones in gonads (which produce cells that, when they are joined with another reproductive cell from a member of the opposite sex of the same species, will grow into an individual). Because of its diverse effects the pituitary gland is often called the master gland.

The hormones produced by the gonads are progestin and estrogen in the female and androgen in the male. The word androgen comes from a Greek word meaning *man* or *male* and is responsible for male appearance and behavior. Likewise, the hormones of the female are responsible for her appearance and behavior.

Too much or too little of a hormone can affect the maleness or femaleness disastrously. Examples of this are the giant, the dwarf, and the bearded lady in the freak show.

Caroline Arnold, in this same book (on page 61), continues on the effects of hormones:

Sex hormones can affect sex differences in 2 ways. They cause permanent changes in developing organs in the brain. They usually occur very early in life, either before or right after birth. The sex hormones also cause temporary changes in behavior or appearance which usually occur late in life and fluctuate depending on hormonal levels. In most animals, genetic sex conception determines the sex of the adult.

Notice the three words *genetic*, *sex* and *conception*. The endocrine glands, this "body computer," secrete the hormones that direct and determine the actions of the other organs and glands in the body which, in turn, determine human behavior to a great, great degree. Much more evidence of this could be presented here, but this author feels that it is not necessary. It is hoped that this has been accepted by the reader.

Different books vary a bit when naming the glands in this system. There are books which include the pineal and the pancreas while others do not. For this study, the organs named in the book *The Human Organism and the World of Life* will be the standard. On page 17 of this book, we find:

The six most important endocrine glands are the islet of Langerhans in the pancreas; the thyroid and parathyroid glands in the neck; the adrenal glands just above the kidneys; the pituitary gland attached to the base of the brain; and the endocrine glands of the sex organs.

Although the interest in this section of this treatise is in the sex glands, something should be said about the others named. Although it is not "spelled out," it is known that all organs of a system play some part in the functioning of each other and the job each is suppose to do to complete the whole. This is especially true with this system.

1. The Pituitary
   A. Size of a pea, has 2 parts;
   B. Produces hormones that affect other glands and organs, including the reproductive organs and adrenal glands; controls ovulation in the female and sperm production in the male. It produces a growth hormone whose underproduction results in dwarfism and overproduction results in giantism, thus it can be said that this gland tells the body when to stop growing.

2. The Adrenal Gland
   A. Produces a small amount of sex hormones which augment those produced by the gonads (ovaries and testes);
   B. Produces adrenalin, which prepares the body to act in dangerous emergencies.

3. The Thyroid (and Parathyroids)
   A. This gland is directed by the hypothalamus (another gland) and a hormone from the pituitary. It produces the hormone thyroxin, which regulates the body's metabolism and heat production, et cetera, thus keeping the bodily functions going the proper rate. The most important job of the parathyroid is to produce parathyroxin to keep an adequate amount of calcium salts in the circulating blood.

4. The Islet of Langerhans
   A. Small groups of cells in the pancreas smaller than pancreas cells;
   B. Secretes insulin (a hormone);
      a. Controls metabolism of carbohydrates;

b. A degeneration of these results in a form of diabetes.

5. The Gonads (Sex Glands)
The hypothalamus controls production of the gonad hormones (ovaries in the female and testes in the male). The testes produce testosterone (and there are some sources that say estrogen also) while the ovaries produce progesterone and estrogen (and there are some that include androgen).

The female hormones are responsible for the release of ova (eggs) and control the menstrual cycle. All of the hormones secreted are responsible for the male characteristics in the male and the female characteristics in the female—the secondary sexual characteristics germane to each sex, generally referred to as masculinity and femininity.

The foregoing is only a "smattering" of the functions and importance of the endocrine system. Endocrinology is a branch of medical science, and it is possible that it could take volumes to explain this system and its importance, for there is much more to be learned, and endocrinologists continue to study it.

The overactivity or the underactivity of any of the glands of the endocrine system causes a marked change or deviation in the development of the parts of the body involved and/or the behavior of the individual and causes many serious diseases.

A case in point is found on pages 230–31 of the book *Hormones, Sex and Happiness.* The writers tell of Annette who developed a tumor of the pituitary gland at the age of twenty-five. First she developed amenorrhea (cessation of menses). Next a new growth of hair on her face caused her to shave several times a week.

In case 2, on page 233, the following is presented.

When Dora was 42 years old, she noticed that her periods were losing regularity. A few months later her feminine curves flattened out, her period ceased, and she began to lose her hair. Though her husband, Allan, jokingly called her his boyfriend, he was really worried about her. When she began to grow a beard and sound like her son on the telephone, there was no longer any reason for treating the situation as a joke. Allan finally convinced her of the advisability of visiting her physician—a suggestion she previously resisted. The unhappy verdict was that she had malignant tumors of both her ovaries that were producing male hormones. Unfortunately, at the time of surgery her tumor had already spread too far and in one year she was dead. When these tumors are benign, simply removing them will allow the woman to become progressively less masculine and once again feminine.

Case 3, on page 233 of the same book, relates:

A more common situation—one we are able to diagnose—is actually a genetic male (testicular feminization). As we have seen in chapter II, when there is damage to the *male gonads*, the fetus develops along feminine lines. In these cases, a male child is conceived, and for reasons probably genetic, the testes do not develop normally. They remain within the abdomen and produce estrogen (female hormone) that performs its usual function—the development of breast tissue and the production of feminine curves. The child grows up as a girl, but fails to have a menstrual period.

Further reading of this book tells of an instance when a doctor was called to the emergency room to see a 29-year-old woman with vaginal bleeding who had had sex for the first time. When he examined her, he found a narrow, short vagina.

A chromosomal study confirmed what he had suspected the lady was a genetic male.

These cases were selected by this writer in order that the reader might see how abnormalities in the body structure or/and in the functioning of the sex glands can easily disturb the femininity or the masculinity of an individual, thus causing a genetic sex different from what the "outside" sex shows.

The above-named book states that this does not mean that these cases are prevalent or not prevalent—only that they are instances that could be found and diagnosed. However, it does give truth to the fact that people do not "choose" their sexuality.

Nothing was said about the sex drive of the individuals in the foregoing cases (as to the "normalcy" or "abnormality" of it) before and after the physical changes wrought by the hormonal changes (imbalance). This writer feels that since one's feelings (sensations) arise from the body tissue when it is stimulated by an impulse carried to and from the brain by one or more sense organs, the condition of the tissue receiving it determines much. However, one cannot say it determines all because of the fact that the response of the body chemistry is an abstract entity.

Dr. Floyd L. Ruch on page 134 of his book *Psychology and Life* has this to say of the sexual urge:

> The sexual drive is second only to the hunger drive in its implications for social living. While our society does not place many elaborate reductions or taboos upon the food-taking behavior of its members, sexual expression is very closely governed both by law and by firmly rooted social conventions. Because our social structure limits an individual's sexual behavior, conscious awareness of the sex urge is more persistent and more insistent than hunger and other drives which are not so likely to go unsatisfied. This socially necessary conflict between the sexual drive and cultural restrictions on its expres-

sion makes one's sex one of the most powerful dynamic forces in human behavior.

Dr. Ruch is quite right in the above quote, especially when he speaks of the socially necessary conflict between the sexual drive and cultural restrictions of its expression. This causes one to wonder if one individual has the right to make laws concerning how another person satisfies that drive as long as the participants are consenting adults. Only the individual himself knows his sexual drive and how to satisfy it. Should he be deprived of this because someone else says he should? Of course, this does not include children or incest.

Chapter V
Complexity of the Development Process

The Beginning of an Individual

When one thinks of the complexity of the process that takes place from the time a sperm penetrates an egg and produces an ovum until nine months later when a complete billion-celled human machine programmed to run and produce other individuals is born, it is easy to see the possibility of something going wrong during that process. This whole process of producing the individual is left to the programming in the ultramicroscopic genes that are locked within the chromosomes. The minute particles, too small for the naked eye to see, must see to it that each part of the body develops as it should, where it should, and when it should. They must cause all of the sense organs to receive stimuli via the nervous system, pass it to the brain that, if developed correctly, can interpret it, and pass it to the correct part of the body that is to react to the stimuli.

Dr. Shyrock (and others) encapsulates much of this in a few words on page 3 of his book, *Modern Medical Guide*, where the following is found:

The genes are composed of DNA, the marvelous protein

substance which controls the form and function of the cells and tissues of a particular individual so that they harmonize with the heredity pattern. The DNA molecules function like a blueprint with every cell in the body having a copy. Thus, every cell's functions are regulated so that billions of cells composing the person's body function cooperatively.

The book *Sex Hormones—Why Males and Females Are Different*, by Caroline Arnold, adds the following from page 57:

> The parts of each living thing that determine its shape, activities, and relationship with other cells are called genes. Each gene is responsible for some characteristic called an inherited trait of that individual. In the human being, genes affect everything from hair and eye color to walking and talking. There are approximately 3000 genes on each chromosome.

After reading all of the foregoing quotes in the preceding chapter and this chapter and taking notes of the emphasis that is put upon inherited traits, one might immediately say, "Yes, but sex is not inherited."

That is true but none of what has been said or will be said is an attempt to prove that sex *per se* is inherited. Only structure is inherited, and thus one must be aware of the fact that all human action is initiated within and performed by the structure, therefore, the condition of this structure is of paramount importance. Its functioning is dependent upon the health, quality, perfectness, and all that the structure brings with it from the parents' parents of the individual that is to be.

With Dr. Shyrock's (and others) explanation below, taken from pages 4 and 5 of the book *Modern Medical Guide*, one will have a good idea of the complexity of the actual "happenings" as the chromosomes make ready to "make" another human being. Here he gives the exact cell action that takes place and explains how the needed numbers are acquired. One can readily understand why of the billions of individuals that populate the planet, there are no two alike when one sees the number of chromosome combinations possible, and Dr. Shyrock lets it be known that in the selection of the chromosomes that are to be eliminated from each pair, it is done purely by chance.

All cells of the human body possess 46 chromosomes each. But we see that if these sex cells continue to possess 46 chromosomes up to the moment new life is conceived, that 46 chromosomes from the mother and 46 from the father would make 92 chromosomes rather than the 46 needed. So nature reduces the number of chromosomes in a then mature sex cell.

Recall that the 46 chromosomes in ordinary cells occur in pairs, there being 23 pairs in each cell. Now, as the sex cells become mature, just before they are available for the initiation of new life, one member of each chromosome pair is eliminated from the cell. *Which member of the pair is thrown out is a matter of chance.* It may be the chromosome that came from the parent's father or the one deviated from his mother at his conception many years before. With 23 pairs present in the cells and with each pair being subject to the laws of chance as to which member is eliminated, it would be very unusual for any 2 sex cells produced by this individual to have the same composition of chromosomes when they become mature.

There are some 281 billion different chromosome combinations possible when the sex cells from a husband and wife unite at time of conception.

When immature sex cells are prepared for the possibility of conception, one member of each pair of chromosomes is eliminated. In the case of the female sex cells, the sex chromosome that is retained will always be an X chromosome because that is the only kind of sex chromosome present in the cells of the female. But in the case of the male sex cells when they are prepared for the possibility of conception some cells will contain an X and some a Y.

During the gestation process we now know that many activities are necessary—selection, timing, placing, forming, developing, producing, et cetera. This begins with the one cell, containing the contribution of the father and the mother, dividing into two cells, the two into four, four into eight, and so on until there is a group of cells of the same kind formed. This takes only a few days after which specialization begins.

Certain cells become modified to form bone, certain to form skin, others to form muscles, others to form the different organ systems, et cetera. From this specialization all tissues and organs of the body come into being bringing along within them a combination of all the traits to be inherited from each parent.

It is during this first two months that the internal sex organs develop to the point that one can tell (microscopically) if the child will be a girl or a boy. The external sex organs develop during the third month.

All the foregoing happens only if the genes have done their job correctly. If a mistake is made, the error will be felt by the individual so affected and, no doubt, it will manifest itself in the overt behavior that emanates from the tissue, be it endogenous or exogenous.

When one recognizes the enormity of the task, the fact that something can go wrong is not surprising and sometimes it does. The surprising thing is that everything goes right so often. There are babies born with birth defects, some of which can be corrected and others that cannot be corrected. Society views with compassion a person affected with a cleft lip, one leg shorter than the other, deafness, blindness, and many other defects. At times the defect is in the brain and interferes with the intellect, which, of course, interferes with the quality of life.

Individuals, companies, and sometimes governments do whatever they can to compensate these unfortunate persons for whatever problems the defects cause them. However, these persons are considered handicapped and looked upon as different from the "norm." But what happens when the difference can't be seen? What happens when it is of a sexual nature?

Society also considers that different from the "norm" (which is true but not physically handicapping) but as for its reaction to it, it is diametrically opposite to what it is for others; it is one of blame. Not only does society blame the persons for the difference, but in some cases they are ostracized by their own families and parents. Many lose their jobs and many experience other shameful absurdities because of society's attitude and complete ignorance.

However, believe it or not, there is a mutuality in the thinking of homosexuals and heterosexuals about each other. To these persons their sexuality is as normal for them as the heterosexuals view their own. Conversely so, heterosexuality is as abnormal for them as theirs is to the heterosexual, and if not persecuted they can lead happy lives, contributing much more to society than many others do. History is replete with the contribution of many, and the culture has profited from this.

As time goes by and advances in science (especially medical science) are made, bringing to the world facts that heretofore were unknown and feats that once seemed impossible, those who today blame will tomorrow understand. In this vein, maybe the prevailing negative attitudes toward homosexuality will become as outdated as the ridiculous and unjust views previously held about the mentally ill and witches. When that happens, society will have made one giant step in its slow trek towards higher intelligence, greater compassion, and complete civilization.

As this chapter comes to a close, it is hoped that the evidence presented is sufficient to negate the belief that homosexuality is a *chosen* way of life. To say that heterosexuals did not and could not choose their sexuality while homosexuals were given a choice and chose their sexuality is a bit absurd, to say the least.

In many instances, in the quotes from the authorities in the field of human biology, there have been overlaps and repetition. This has been necessary because of the context in which it was used. In none of the material has anyone mentioned that the sex drive or body chemistry might be different in people affected. So, before the close of this chapter, information about the field of genetics is needed.

Genetics The branch of biology dealing with heredity and variations in animals and plants.
—*Webster's American Dictionary for Home, School and Office*, Glen Ellen, Ill.: Paramount Publishers, Inc., 1970.

From the book *Human Genetics*, by Norman V. Rothwell, professor of biology at Long Island University, this explanation helps one to understand more about hormones and their workings.

When the human chromosomes are paired and systematically arranged according to size and shape, seven groups can be recognized. The chromosome's complement of any cell is called its karyotype. A normal human karyotype includes 46 chromosomes or 23 pairs. In the female every chromosome has a homologue which corresponds to it exactly in size and shape. The same is true for the male except for one pair, the sex chromosomes. These 2 chromosomes of the male are distinctly different in appearances: a large X and a Y. In the female two

X chromosomes are present and the Y is absent. All the chromosomes in a cell other than the sex chromosomes are called autosome—a human male thus has 22 pairs of autosome plus one X and one Y.

On page 40 of this same book we find this:

> ...just like any other creature, the human will suffer some sort of abnormality if there is a departure from the karyotype which is typical for the male and female of the human species.
> ...the consequences in the human of departure from the normal chromosome complement or karyotype present a real and significant problem not only to the geneticist and the medical person but to society as a whole.

This writer could go on quoting Norman V. Rothwell as to the possibility, and the fact, that abnormalities do exist in the sexual area. Of course this predisposes a person to a deviation from what America calls "normal sex," but to the person affected, it is normal for him. It's a homosexual's only way of sexual satisfaction.

If one reads his marvelous book one will find in chapter IV—entitled "Sex Chromosomes and the Genes They Carry"—and the subtopic—"Abnormalities of Sex Hormones"—*that one no longer has to question whether or not homosexuality is of the body or of the mind. This chapter alone establishes the fact that the body is the culprit (if that word can be used).*

In this chapter, the author does not mention the term homosexuality, but he solidly establishes the fact that there are abnormalities in the chromosomes (and answers question number 1 in chapter 2). Special attention should be paid to page 77 and the last two sentences in the first paragraph that read:

An extra Y obviously permits the initiation of masculine development and does not interfere with its completion. An extra X along with the Y, however, will result in feminization probably by causing in some way a reduction in the effectiveness of the male hormone.

The answer to question 2 is yes, the chromosome can cause abnormalities and thus produce sexes that are not absolute, but mixtures.

One will find on page 71 the following:

The importance of an XX or XY constitution to normal sex is seen in those cases where the number of sex chromosomes departs from the typical. At times in humans as well as in other species, individuals arise with a karyotype which possesses some alterations in the number of chromosomes or chromosome structure.

The author speaks of Down's syndrome, which comes from an extra autosome, chromosome number 21. He continues:

Among American babies born each year, approximately 20,000 will have some kind of disorder or effect due directly to some type of chromosome aberrations.

Chapter VI
Summary and Conclusion

Very often when homosexuality is discussed in the presence of most heterosexuals, feelings that are aroused are those of negativity and repulsion. No doubt, this is based on what they have been told and not from a study of human biology and genetics—or, for that matter, a study of any science whose facts come from research, study, and experimentation. To those who believe otherwise it connotes 1) sex between two persons of the same sex, 2) an expression of sex that they themselves have "chosen," 3) they are sick people and it's all in the mind, and 4) they can be "cured" but refuse to do so because of their "low morals."

Needless to say, none of the above is true. The truth or falsity of it is evident in the preceding chapters of this treatise. This evidence comes from authorities in their respective fields (said before); examples of cases found in which hormonal imbalances have changed the physical characteristics of the opposite sex; that all traits are carried on the genes in the hormones (including sex); that sex is determined at the time of conception (when the X or Y chromosome of the male penetrates the female egg with its X chromosome); that sex cannot be changed, that sex change operations are not really sex changes but operations to bring out the sex that is already there for those whose sex has been misjudged at birth.

Love in the gay community is the same as in the nongay community as far as the female is concerned. With them it is not characterized by the promiscuity characteristic of males. Pre-AIDS promiscuity is legendary, but this does not refer to all gay men, and heterosexual men are also promiscuous. However, because his partner is female, he is restricted to a degree by the female who, in our society, is labeled a nymphomaniac and a "tramp" if she is promiscuous.

The "set of rules" to which our nation is supposed to adhere is not the one used in many other countries. For example, in one country (and there may be others) it is said that gay couples are allowed to marry. The book *The Reproduction of Life*, by Robert L. Lehrman, has this to say:

> How one views different processes varies greatly in different cultures. In many cultures girls (and in some instances, boys) are expected to be virgins when they marry. A Polynesian girl is not considered a good catch until she has proven her fertility by having a baby. Homosexuality is a crime and a disgrace in America. In ancient Greece it was the most exalted form of sexual activity and in some cultures—a sign of a mystic gift.

Homosexuality and bisexuality are nothing new. They have existed since life on earth began. The book *Sex Hormones—Why Males and Females Are Different*, by Caroline Arnold, tells us that it exists in the animal world (this writer has seen it) and speaks of the anemone, a fish that has both male and female sex organs and can function as either male or female.

Neither does homosexuality nor bisexuality exist in isolated cases. Because of the stigma that American society places upon this and the way it treats people of this orientation, many spend a lifetime keeping this part of their lives a secret. It was only in the 60s that the younger uninhibited generation began to "come out of the closet" and demand their rights. This could not have been done earlier and even now many suffer discrimination and ostracism from their work places, their families, and former friends. Below are expressions by persons interviewed in the 60s self-emancipation.

1. We must keep our love hidden and for our entire lives live an open life and a hidden life. We walk the back roads in our love lives regardless of how sincere and dedicated to humanity we are, when all the while the heterosexual no matter how promiscuous, criminal or "dirty" and obnoxious, can walk the main streets. He may be a murderer or rapist, but he is accepted by many if pardoned or his term of incarceration is completed.

2. One of the most traumatic experiences I've ever experienced was when I discovered I was homosexual with a body chemistry that reacted to "my own" sex and I couldn't react to the opposite sex.

Another person interviewed stated that it came to him naturally and it did not bother him until he was subjected to the taboos of society and the scorn of his own family and childhood friends. The people of this sexual orientation want the same as those who are not—a love that they can show to the world, the ability to marry and choose to have children and become a solid citizen in one's community, but society says they cannot. Often they marry because they have been told it will "cure" them, but very soon they learn that they cannot adjust and the repulsiveness of the hetero-physical sex is more than they can take and continue to force themselves to do. With the bisexual, both lives can be led—one in the light, and one in the dark.

It seems to be the thinking of society that the gay community is a group apart from the people with whom they associate, but this is not true. There are millions of people of this orientation, and they are among the people one sees every day, those with whom one works, sits beside in church, mingles with in clubs, organizations, and all affairs public or private. They are doctors, lawyers, ministers, priests, politicians, your acquaintances, your friends, and your relatives. Contrary to belief, they will not assault you or make passes at you. (Watch for that from the heterosexual.) Just as heterosexuals do not want all persons of the opposite sex that they see, neither do gay people want all of the "same sex" they see. Many heterosexuals flatter themselves in thinking this.

Just as many of them are devout Christians and their relationship with God is sincere; their belief is deep; they lead Christian lives, and would not dare stoop to some of the things that some nongay people do or treat others as some of them treat gays. They live quiet lives and reach out to help their fellowman. In other words, there are many in this community who are better people than the heterosexuals who scorn them, mistreat them, try to deny them their rights, and consider them immoral.

It is true that many have tired of the life of secrecy and have "come out of the closet," some with such attitudes as

1. Why should I hide my sexuality?
2. It came to me just as it came to the heterosexuals.
3. I did not choose it any more than the homosexuals chose theirs, and it is just as normal to me as theirs are to them.
4. I have just as much right to satisfy my sexual drive with a consenting mate as the homosexual has to satisfy his.
5. Regardless of his law that says I must have his kind of sex when that is not what my body calls for, I will not let him legislate my sex.
6. We (two consenting adults) have as much right to satisfy our sexual drive as he has to satisfy his, even if he blames me for my drive.
7. I did not make myself and if society wants to blame anyone, blame the one who made me—God.

As we close this part of our book, just as when we began it, there are questions to be asked, but the main ones are these.

1. Can a country legislate sex between two consenting adults done in privacy?
2. Can two citizens be jailed for satisfying their sex drive in the only way they can just because it is not the way others satisfy theirs?
3. Does the heterosexual satisfy his drive in the way he does because it is considered "normal" and society accepts it, or does he do this because it satisfies? (The answer to this is known.)
4. In America (which boasts of its freedom, "preaches" to the world about human rights; hesitates to test people [such as pilots], for drug use who hold the safety of other people in their hands; hesitates to search students' lockers in schools in an attempt to save youth from drugs; and hesitates to test for the AIDS virus in an attempt to stymie a national killing epidemic because it is considered an invasion of privacy), should the government have the right to go in a person's bedroom, arrest and jail him because the kind of sex it finds there is not what the law says it should be?
5. What is more private than sex?
6. How long will it be before someone tests the constitutionality of such a law?

Just as was said of the answers in one of Bob Dylan's song's lyrics, the answers to the above questions are also "blowing in the wind."

Bibliography

Arnold, Caroline, *Sex Hormones: Why Males and Females Are Different.* New York: William Morrow and Co., 1981.

Connel, Elizabeth B., M.D., Joseph E. Davis, M.D., and Joseph W. Goldzieher, M.D. *Hormones, Sex and Happiness.* Cowles Book Co., 1971.

The Holy Bible, King James Version.

The Human Body: The Endocrine System. New York; Tostar Books.

Lehr, Robert L. *The Reproduction of Life.* New York: Man Basic Books, Inc.

The New Standard Encyclopedia, vol. 3. Chicago: Standard Education Society, Inc., 1957.

Rothwell, Norman V. *Human Genetics.* Englewood Cliffs: Prentice-Hall Publishing Co., 1977.

Ruch, Floyd L. *Psychology and Life.* Chicago: Scott, Foresman, and Co.

Shyrock, Harold, M.D., èt al. *Modern Medical Guide.* Mountain View: Pacific Press Pub. Assoc., 1979.

Young, Clarence W. *The Human Organism and the World of Life.* New York: Harper and Brothers, 1938.